D1309753

STICKA-PIX

IN THE OCEAN

Create amazing pictures one sticker at a time!

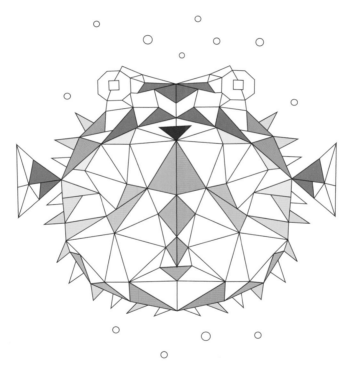

Illustrated by Michael Buxton
Written by Karen Gordon Seed

BARRON'S

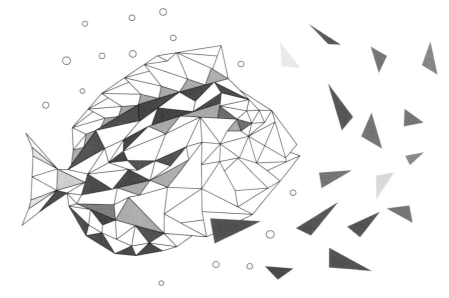
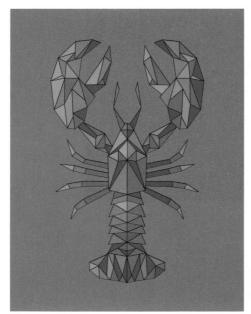

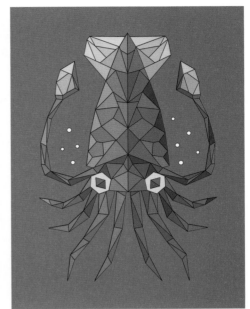

STICKA-PIX

Create amazing pictures one sticker at a time. Simply match the stickers to the correct shape, position them on the page, and add color to create your Sticka-Pix masterpieces!

To find the correct stickers, match the number on the reference picture on the left of each page to its corresponding number on the sticker pages. Use the spare white stickers wherever you choose.

Not all shapes have stickers, so you will need to use colored pencils to help you complete each picture.

Turtle

There are seven species of sea turtle, whose ancestors roamed Earth with the dinosaurs 110 million years ago. They have a long life span of up to 80 years. Sea turtles spend most of their lives in the sea and can stay under water for up to five hours by slowing their heart rate to conserve oxygen.

Pufferfish

To defend themselves, pufferfish inflate their bodies using air or water so that they become entirely round. They slowly return to normal once danger has passed. Many species are poisonous and when eaten, particularly in Japan, they must be prepared by specially trained chefs to avoid death!

Great White Shark

Great whites are the most feared and powerful predatory sharks in the world. They have existed in their current species for 18 million years! Every single tooth is designed to cut into flesh and can easily shatter bone. When threatened, sharks' eyes roll back in their heads for protection.

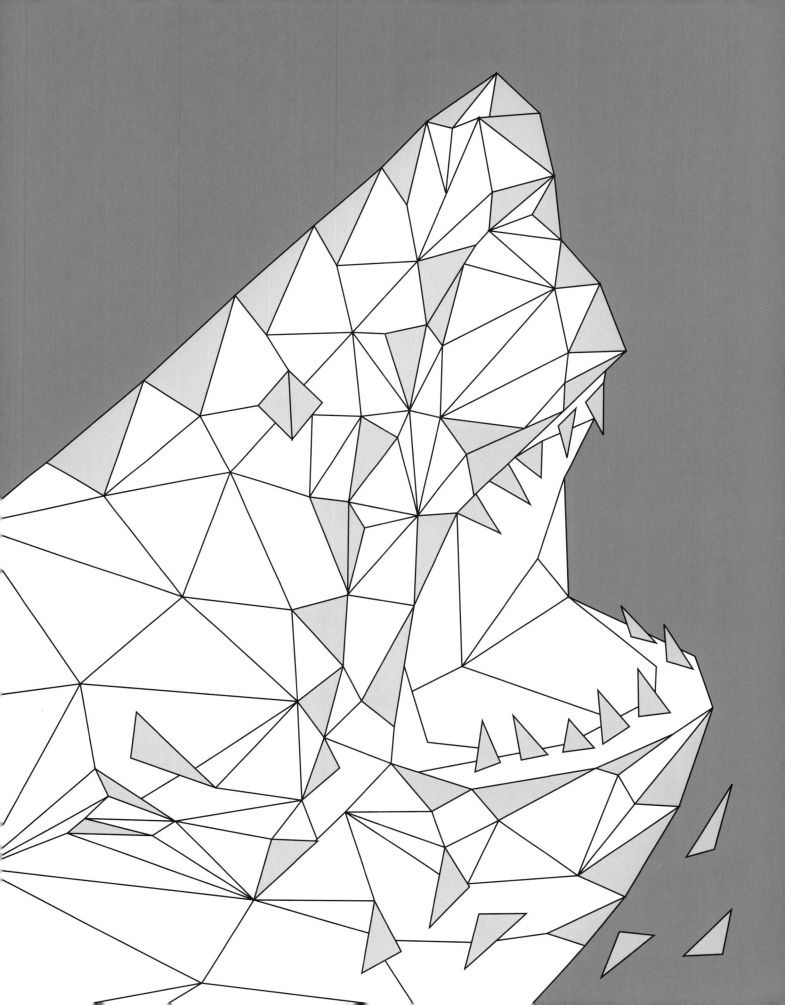

Blue Tang

Blue tang play an important role in the life cycle of coral reefs, where they use their small, sharp teeth to feed on excess algae, cleaning the reef and preventing coral from suffocating. Unlike the dazzlingly blue adults, young tangs have bright yellow skin with blue spots near their eyes.

Jellyfish

Jellyfish are one of the most sophisticated and adaptable creatures on Earth. They can live in both cold and warm seas, and survive in waters both shallow and deep. A jellyfish uses its tentacles to stun prey before gobbling it up through its mouth in the center of its body.

Giant Squid

Giant squid live deep in the oceans and are very elusive, meaning little is known about them. What we do know is that they have the largest eyes in the animal kingdom. Each one measures a huge 10 inches (25 cm) in diameter, allowing squid to see in the dark depths more than most other creatures.

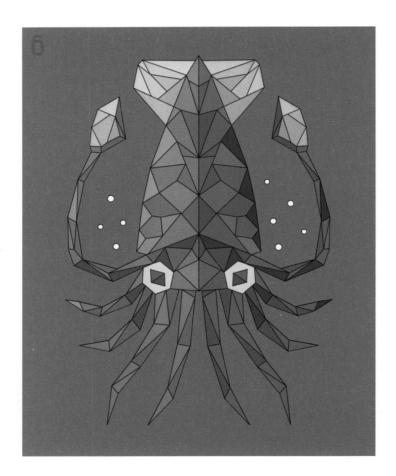

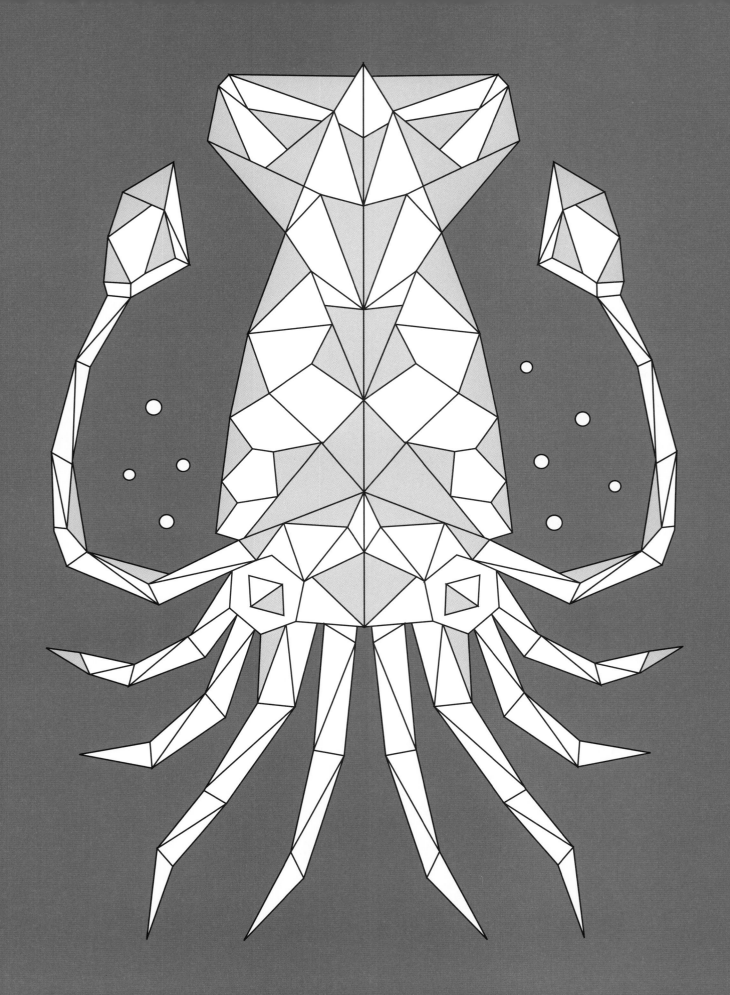

Anemonefish

Anemonefish, or "clownfish," are so named because of the multicolored sea anemones where they live. Found in the Pacific and Indian oceans, clownfish reside in warm, shallow reefs. Before taking up residence, a clownfish will form a layer of mucus that's resistant to the anemone's sting.

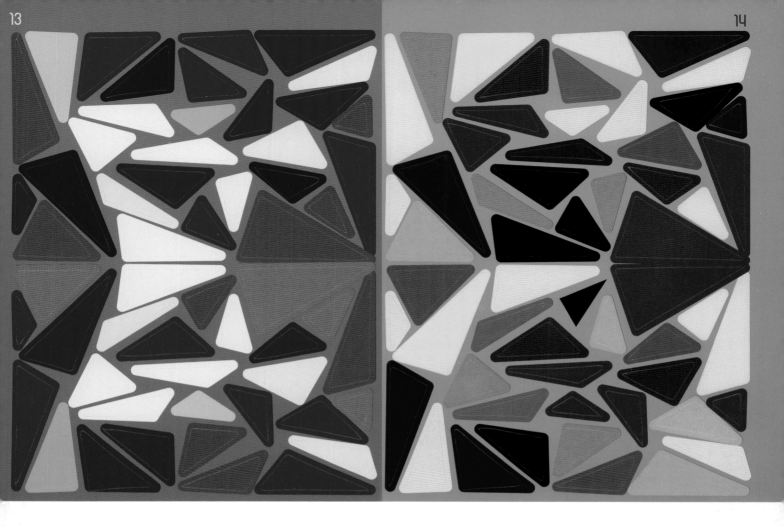

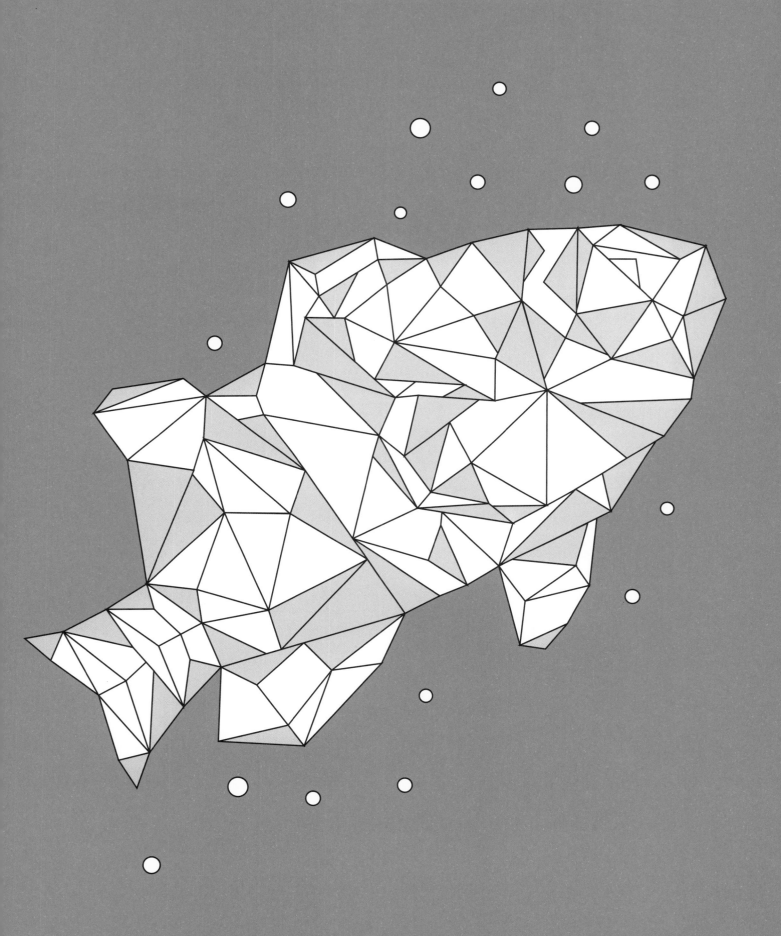

Orca

Orcas are the world's largest species of dolphin. They live in large family groups in cold coastal and polar waters, and each orca can live from 50 to 80 years in the wild. Clever and deadly, orcas hunt in groups, or "pods," searching for fish, seals, squid, and seabirds.

Lobster

Lobsters are 10-legged crustaceans that can grow up to 3 feet (1 m) in length. They can be found in all the world's oceans, and in freshwater, too. Lobsters feed on fish and mollusks, and some will eat other lobsters. They have to shed their shells in order to grow, and can live up to 50 years.

Walrus

Walruses are very social creatures, spending their days lying on the Arctic ice, bellowing and snorting at one another. Their iconic features are very practical: their blubbery flesh keeps them warm, their whiskers detect food in the water, and they use their tusks to defend and attack.

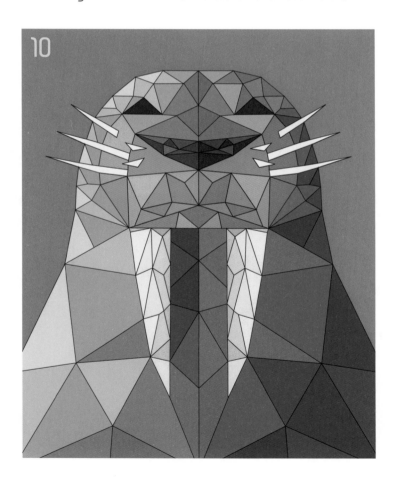

Seahorse

Every morning, paired seahorses meet to reinforce their bond with a dance of courtship. During this display, each seahorse will change color. In fact, seahorses can change their color at any time to fit in with their surroundings. To eat, they suck up food in their snouts like a vacuum cleaner.

11

Anglerfish

At the bottom of the sea, you'll find the strange anglerfish. The females, who are much larger than the males, can eat prey twice their size because of their huge mouths and bodies. An anglerfish uses its dorsal spine like a glow-in-the-dark fishing rod luring prey across the dark ocean depths.

12

Manta Ray

Manta rays live in warm seas and swim by using their wing-like fins to propel themselves through the water. Rays can often be seen leaping through the surface. They feed on plankton and small fish, which are swept into their mouths by front, cephalic fins that look like devil's horns.

13

Dolphin

Dolphins are particularly intelligent, with excellent eyesight and hearing, along with the ability to use echolocation to find food and other dolphins. They live in family groups called "pods," where they interact and play. To communicate, they use a variety of sounds, whistles, and clicks.

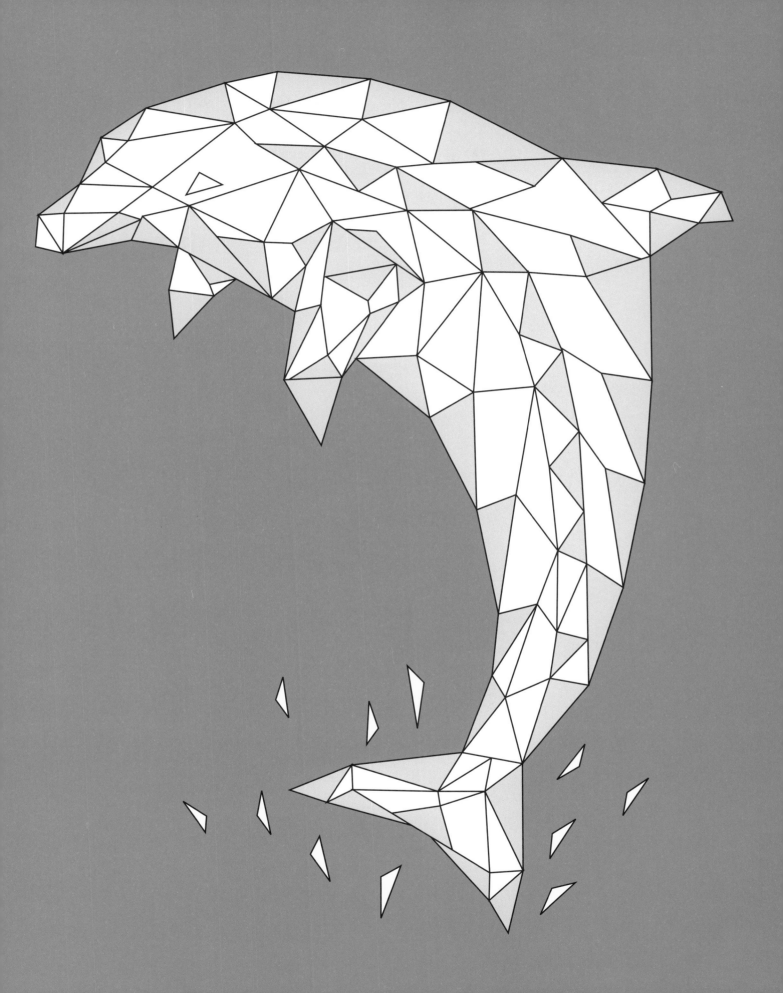